RAISING MENTALLY STRONG KIDS

WORKBOOK

+ TIPS FOR GRANDPARENTS

DANIEL G. AMEN, MD

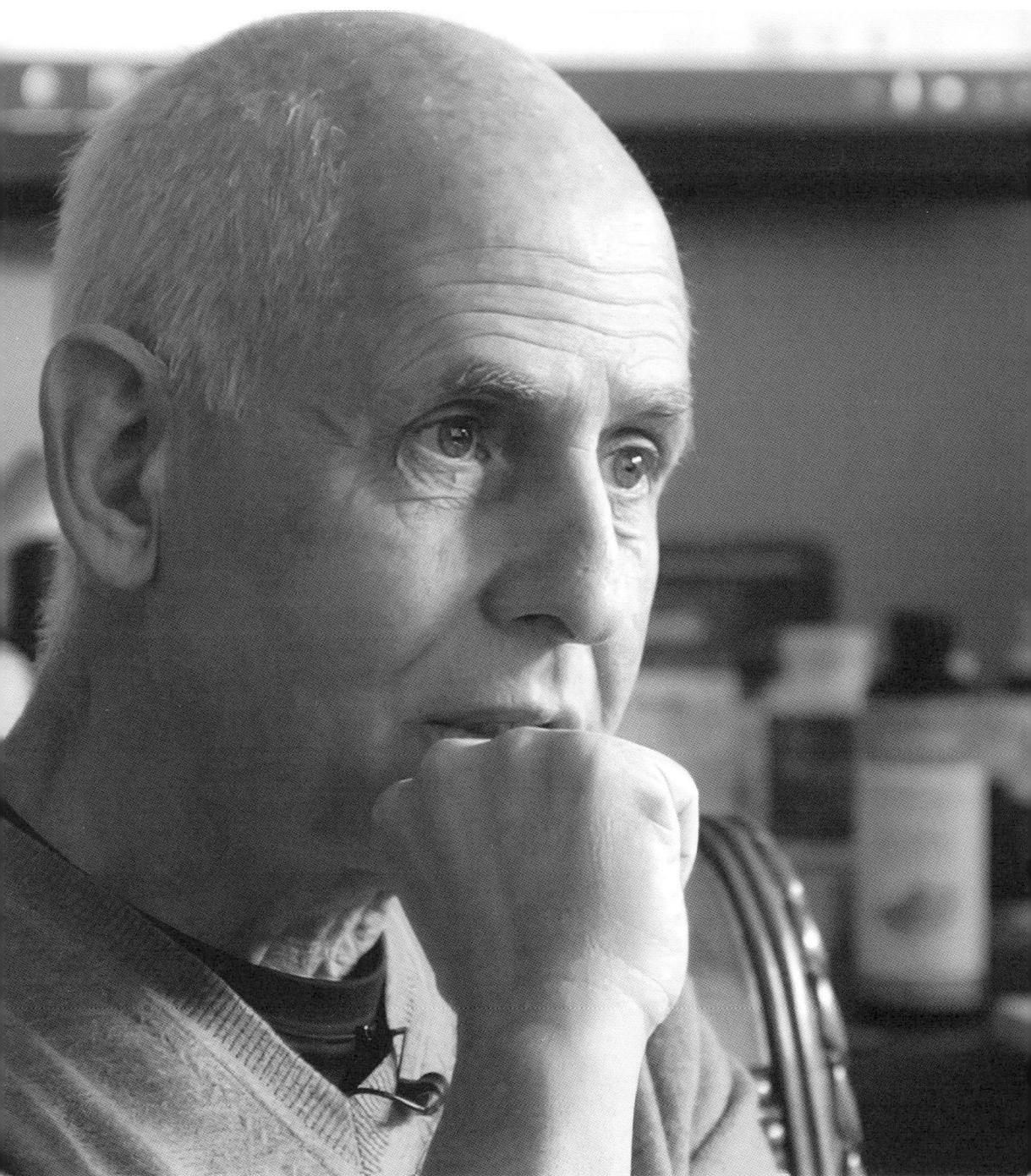

CONTENTS

INTRODUCTION

Parenting is the most important job there is, and raising children to be mentally strong so they grow into respectful, competent, kind, and successful adults is no easy feat. For more than three decades at Amen Clinics, I have had the honor of working with thousands of people who are raising kids.

Parents, grandparents, and other caregivers have come to me with tears of frustration, feelings of failure, or children whose behavior was so out of control they were at a complete loss about what to do. But I assured them there was hope, and I worked closely with them to help shift some of their parenting practices that were fueling a lot of the problems.

The strategies I teach my patients are the same ones I am sharing with you in this workbook and are based on the 7 Core Conversations I have had with parents, grandparents, and other caregivers for more than 30 years.

By making changes to ineffective or unhealthy parenting practices, I have witnessed many people help their children overcome behavior problems, bad attitudes, a sense of entitlement, school failure, social problems, poor self-esteem, and more. The strategies they learned to incorporate also helped their children become more confident, respectful, healthier, and mentally stronger.

These positive changes made parenting easier and each household a happier and more pleasant place to be. I want the same benefits for you and your family too, and this workbook will help you achieve just that.

Here's to more mentally strong children of the future!

Daniel G. Amen, MD

GETTING THE MOST FROM THIS WORKBOOK

I know you want to be the best parent possible so your children can become mentally strong as they grow up, so they have the best chances of success in all aspects of their lives. This workbook will help you do just that.

In it you will learn and practice the key tenets of the 7 Core Conversations for Raising Mentally Strong Kids—the same ones that I have had with thousands of parents, grandparents, and other caregivers during the past three decades.
The conversations are these:

> Core Conversation #1. Brain Health is Foundational to Mental Strength
> Core Conversation #2. Focused Intention
> Core Conversation #3. Bonding—You Have No Influence Without Connection
> Core Conversation #4. The Brain Needs Boundaries
> Core Conversation #5. Teach Your Kids How to Solve Their Own Problems
> Core Conversation #6. Notice What You Like About Your Kids Way More Than What You Don't
> Core Conversation #7. Get Kids Help Early When They Need It

I recommend you read and complete the exercises in the order they appear, because each conversation chapter builds on the previous one.

For the sake of brevity in this workbook, the term "parent" refers to anyone who is in that role, whether you are a biological or adoptive parent, step-parent, grandparent, or relative raising a family member's child. It also applies to any other type of caregiver. The information and strategies in this workbook are also very helpful for teachers, counselors, coaches, guardians, and others who are involved in helping children become mentally strong.

Now, let's get started!

CORE CONVERSATION #1

IF YOU WANT YOUR KIDS AND GRANDKIDS TO BE MENTALLY STRONG, IT STARTS BY BUILDING A HEALTHY BRAIN.

Brain health is the foundation of being mentally strong. However, it is often the missing link in children who struggle.

For more than three decades at Amen Clinics, we have used a type of brain imaging technology (SPECT) that looks at blood flow and activity. From the more than 250,000 scans in our database, we have learned that most psychiatric illnesses are not mental health issues, rather they are brain health problems that steal your mind.

Learning how to love and care for your brain—and teaching your children to do the same—can be a game changer for your family that enhances mental fortitude.
Learn and practice the following seven principles to optimize brain function for yourself and your loved ones.

7 BRAIN PRINCIPLES FOR PARENTS AND KIDS

Brain Principle #1
Your brain is involved in everything you do.

Parents: Write down at least three things your brain does:

_____

_____

_____

_____

_____

_____

_____

_____

_____

Ask Your Kids: What are some things your brain helps you do every day?

_____

_____

_____

_____

_____

_____

_____

_____

Brain Principle #2
When your brain works right, you work right. When your brain is troubled, you have trouble in your life.

If your brain isn't working well, which of these could have caused a problem for you and/or your children?

- ☐ Concussions or other head injuries
- ☐ Eating fast food or processed foods
- ☐ Eating/drinking too much sugar
- ☐ Exposure to toxins (i.e. drugs, alcohol, black mold)
- ☐ Having a hangover
- ☐ Not getting enough sleep
- ☐ Skipping breakfast
- ☐ Too much screen time
- ☐ Untreated mental health issues (i.e. depression)

When your brain works well, which healthy behaviors (such as exercise, healthy foods, quality sleep, etc.) have helped you feel your best?

_____

_____

_____

_____

_____

_____

_____

_____

_____

Brain Principle #3
Your brain is the most amazing organ in the universe.

Your brain weighs about 3 pounds and has about 100 billion neurons (nerve cells) and more connections than there are stars in the universe.

Parents: Write down a few things you think are amazing about your brain:

_____

_____

_____

_____

_____

_____

Ask Your Kids: What are some amazing things about your brain? Write it down here:

_____

_____

_____

_____

_____

_____

Brain Principle #4
You need to fall in love with your brain and develop brain envy.

Why do you think this is important?

_____

_____

_____

_____

_____

_____

How can you help your children understand the importance of this concept?

_____

_____

_____

_____

_____

_____

Brain Principle #5
Many things hurt the brain. Avoid them.

The "brain-imaging" work we have done at Amen Clinics has helped us identify the 11 major risk factors that cause harm to the brain. If you have any of these risk factors, parenting may be even more difficult.

If your child has any of these risk factors, then the mental strength, resilience, and focus they need for success in life may elude them.

We developed the mnemonic **BRIGHT MINDS** to help you remember the 11 major risk factors.

'B' is for Blood Flow.

The blood flow to your brain supplies the oxygen and vital nutrients it needs to function optimally. Low blood flow is associated with many problems, including difficulty with focus, mood issues, addictions, and others that can affect people of all ages, including kids, adolescents, teens, and young adults.

Which of these common risk factors for low blood flow apply to you or your children?

- ☐ Exercising less than twice a week
- ☐ Drinking more than two cups of caffeinated drinks a day
- ☐ Hypertension or prehypertension
- ☐ Abnormally low blood pressure
- ☐ History of cardiovascular disease
- ☐ Other blood vessel problems

'R' is for Rational Thinking.

Every thought you have triggers the release of chemicals in your brain that impact its function. When you have positive thoughts, your brain releases neurotransmitters that help you feel good. Conversely, when you have negative thoughts chemicals that can hurt your brain are released. If your brain is infested with automatic negative thoughts (ANTs), they can make you feel miserable.

Which of these risk factors could be interfering with rational thinking for you or your child?

- ☐ Anxiety
- ☐ "Black-and-white thinking"
- ☐ Depression
- ☐ Name calling
- ☐ Self-esteem problems
- ☐ Tendency to be critical of others or self

'I' is for Inflammation.

High levels of inflammation cause harm to the organs in your body, including your brain. And young children who have chronic systemic inflammation can be at risk for problems with brain development.

Do you or your child have any of these issues that could be related to elevated inflammation?

- ☐ Allergies
- ☐ Lack of motivation
- ☐ Leaky gut that causes gastrointestinal issues
- ☐ Mood problems
- ☐ Periodontal (gum) disease

'G' is for Genetics.

Yes, brain health and mental health problems often run in families. But do you know that your genes are not your destiny? Your daily habits—and the ones you teach your children—have bearing on whether those genes get turned off or on.

Check the box(es) next to any of these health problems that tend to run in your family:

- ☐ Alzheimer's disease or other type of dementia
- ☐ Cancer
- ☐ Diabetes
- ☐ Heart disease
- ☐ High blood pressure

☐ High cholesterol
☐ Obesity

'H' is for Head Trauma.

Because the brain is so soft and the skull is very hard with many sharp bony ridges on the inside, even mild concussions and head injuries that occur at any age can contribute to a host of challenging conditions, including:

- Anxiousness
- Difficulty with focus
- Learning problems
- Mood issues
- Vulnerability for abusing alcohol or drugs

Despite common misconceptions, you don't have to lose consciousness for a brain injury to occur. Mark any of the common scenarios for head trauma below that apply to you or your child(ren).

☐ Being in an automobile accident
☐ Head-to-head collisions in sports
☐ Falling out of a tree or off the jungle gym
☐ Being hit on the head by a falling object
☐ Getting punched in the head or face
☐ Crashing on a bicycle, snowboard, skateboard, or other recreational equipment
☐ Getting whiplash
☐ Seeing stars or "getting your bell rung"

'T' is for Toxins.

Environmental toxins are harmful to the brain, yet they seem to be ubiquitous, even in everyday items. Children's developing brains are especially vulnerable to toxins, and exposure to them has been linked to brain fog, learning problems, autism, ADHD, and other issues. Unfortunately, many people are unaware of the places toxins can hide.

Which of these toxins are you or your kids potentially being exposed to?

☐ Alcohol
☐ Cigarettes and/or second-hand smoke
☐ Heavy metals (lead, cadmium, mercury, arsenic, or aluminum)
☐ Mold

- ☐ Nonorganic produce
- ☐ Paint
- ☐ Personal care products (such as some cosmetics and sunscreens)
- ☐ Pesticides
- ☐ Recreational or illicit drugs
- ☐ Smoke

'M' is for Mental Health.

Not only do mental health problems make it more difficult to be an effective parent, but they also make it more challenging for children to do well in school, with friends, and in life. This is why it is so critical to reach out for help as soon as possible—for yourself or your child if you or another loved one has concerns. By doing so, you increase the chances for living a healthy, meaningful, and productive life.

Which of these common mental health problems are affecting you, your child, or other family members?

- ☐ ADHD
- ☐ Anxiety
- ☐ Autism spectrum disorder
- ☐ Behavioral problems
- ☐ Bipolar disorder
- ☐ Chronic stress
- ☐ Childhood trauma
- ☐ Depression
- ☐ Eating disorders
- ☐ Schizophrenia
- ☐ Substance abuse (including alcohol)
- ☐ Traumatic experiences in adulthood

'I' is for Immune System Problems and Infections.

When your immune system is out of balance, you can become more vulnerable to infections that increase your risk for brain fog and memory issues as well as mental health problems. And, some children who get certain infections, such as mononucleosis, strep, Lyme disease, or COVID, may go on to develop neuropsychiatric issues.

Are you or your child struggling with any of these conditions?

☐ Asthma
☐ Cold sores or other herpes infection
☐ Chronic Lyme disease
☐ Crohn's disease
☐ Long COVID
☐ Lupus
☐ Multiple sclerosis
☐ Rheumatoid arthritis
☐ Severe psoriasis
☐ Other autoimmune disorder or untreated chronic infection:

_____

'N' is for Neurohormone Issues.

Hormone imbalances can negatively affect brain function. For example, many people do not know that problems with concentration and paying attention, fatigue, or feeling fuzzy-headed can be related to thyroid problems. Unfortunately these issues might be misdiagnosed as mental health disorders.

The following hormone imbalances mostly affect adults, but they can also occur in kids or teens. If left untreated, they can impact your ability to parent effectively. See if any of these apply to you or your child:

☐ Low estrogen
☐ Low testosterone (in males and females)
☐ Low progesterone
☐ Thyroid that is too high or too low

'D' is for Diabesity.

The word diabesity is a combination of diabetes and obesity, both of which are serious conditions that decrease the size and function of your brain. Diabesity is a significant and widespread problem in the U.S. and other countries.

- Nearly 42% of adults in the U.S are classified as obese—a body mass index (BMI) of 30 or higher.
- 19.7% of U.S. children, including some as young as 2 years old, are obese.

Diabesity causes increased inflammation, systemic blood vessel problems, and a host of other medical ailments. It also can lead to:

- Difficulty with focus
- Learning issues
- Memory problems
- Moodiness and irritability

Mark the diabesity risk factors below that are affecting you and/or your child:

- ☐ Excessive consumption of sugar and high-glycemic foods
- ☐ Sedentary lifestyle
- ☐ Exposure to toxins
- ☐ Family history of diabetes
- ☐ Obesity
- ☐ Metabolic syndrome
- ☐ Alcohol abuse

If you're concerned about diabesity in your family, ask your doctor and pediatrician what the BMI scores are for your family members and record them here.

BMI of parent(s): _____ _____

BMI of children: _____ _____ _____

Compare your numbers to the chart below and mark which category each person is in.

Category	Parent(s)	Child	Child	Child
Obese (>30)				
Overweight (>25-30)				
Normal (>18.5-24.9)				
Underweight (<18.5)				

Body Mass Index Ranges
'S' is for Sleep.

In order to stay healthy, the brain needs an adequate amount of sleep each night, but getting less than seven hours a night has been associated with higher risk of:

- ADHD
- Anxiety
- Brain fog
- Dementia
- Depression

And sleep is critical for developing brains! A lack of sleep is especially hard on teenagers. Some research has found that high school kids who got just one hour less sleep on weekdays resulted in a significant increase in hopelessness, chances of substance abuse, suicidal thoughts, and attempted suicides.

Which Sleep Risk Factors Do You or Your Child Have?

- ☐ Depression
- ☐ Hormonal imbalances
- ☐ Insomnia
- ☐ Poor sleep hygiene (such as too much screen time late into the night)
- ☐ Shift work
- ☐ Sleep apnea

Brain Principle #6
Many things help the brain. Engage in regular brain-healthy habits.

There are so many ways to help your brain—even if you have been bad to it! Here are the BRIGHT MINDS strategies you can use to minimize your and your child's risk factors.

'B' is for Blood Flow:
Strategies for healthy blood flow include:

- Engage in physical exercise for 30 minutes a day.
- Practice meditation and/or prayer.
- Eat foods such as pomegranates, citrus fruit, and walnuts (they increase blood flow).

Which of these are you already doing?

_____

Which of these will you start today?

_____

'R' is for Rational Thinking.
Learning to challenge your automatic negative thoughts (ANTs)—and teaching your children to challenge theirs—can improve self-confidence, reduce sensitivity to constructive criticism, and improve resilience when faced with obstacles.

What strategy are you currently using to challenge your negative self-thoughts?

_____

In the workbook section Core Conversation #6, you'll learn how to use my simple and effective strategy to replace automatic negative thoughts with more accurate and realistic thinking habits.

'I' is for Inflammation.
These strategies help keep inflammation in check:
1. Eat an anti-inflammatory diet, including more foods high in omega-3 fatty acids (such as salmon).
2. Take supplements, such as fish oil and probiotics, and give them to your kids too!
3. Floss your teeth (and teach your children to do so) every day.

Which of these are you already doing?

_____

Which of these will you start today?

_____

'G' is for Genetics.

If you have a family history of mental health conditions, behavioral issues, or memory problems in your family, use these strategies to address your genetic risk factors:

- Get serious about brain health as soon as possible.
- Get screened for any potential problems early.
- Watch for any signs of trouble in your children.
- Know your family's risk factors and work to prevent them every day.

Which of these are you already doing?

_____

Which of these will you start today?

_____

'H' is for Head Trauma.

These strategies are critical for protecting your (and your child's) head to prevent concussions and brain injuries:

1. Always wear a seat belt when in a motor vehicle.
2. Always wear a helmet when biking, skiing, skateboarding, etc.
3. Avoid climbing ladders.
4. Don't head soccer balls.
5. Don't let kids play contact sports like tackle football.
6. Hold the handrails when going up or down stairs.
7. Never text while walking or driving.

Which of these are you already doing?

_____

Which of these will you start today?

_____

'T' is for Toxins.

Strategies to help you avoid exposure to toxins include:

- Download one of several apps available, such as Think Dirty, to help identify common toxins in your household, personal care, and beauty products.
- Don't use self-care products that contain toxins, such as oxybenzone in sunscreen or parabens in cosmetics.
- Eat organic food whenever possible.
- Avoid alcohol, marijuana, and cigarettes.
- Test for mold if you suspect it might be in your home.
- Support the body's four organs of detoxification:
  - Kidneys: Drink more water.
  - Gut: Eat more fiber and choose organic foods.
  - Liver: Quit smoking and avoid drugs, limit alcohol, and eat brassicas (cabbage, broccoli, cauliflower, and Brussels sprouts).
  - Skin: Exercise vigorously enough to sweat.

Which of these are you already doing?

_____

Which of these will you start today?

_____

'M' is for Mental Health.

Use these strategies to improve mental health issues:

- Adopt brain-healthy habits.
- Eliminate your automatic negative thoughts, or ANTs (see Core Conversation #6).
- Get daily physical exercise.
- Practice stress-management techniques.
- increase intake of omega-3 fatty acids.

Which of these are you already doing?

_____

Which of these will you start today?

_____

'I' is for Immune System Problems and Infections.
Strategies to boost immunity and reduce the risk of infections include:

- Check vitamin D levels, and if they are low, get more sun or take a supplement.
- Eat more immune-boosting foods like onions, mushrooms, and garlic.
- Get screened for common infections.
- Treat any infections in yourself or your child early.

Which of these are you already doing?
_____

Which of these will you start today?
_____

'N' is for Neurohormone Issues.
Use these strategies to address any neurohormone issues:

- Test and optimize your hormone levels if you're an adult.
- Avoid hormone disruptors for you and your kids, such as:
  - Certain food products
  - Pesticides
  - Some personal care products

Which of these are you already doing?
_____

Which of these will you start today?
_____

'D' is for Diabesity.
These three basic strategies can help prevent problems with obesity and diabetes for you and your children.

1. Eliminate or limit sugar.
2. Eat a brain-healthy diet.
3. Don't eat more calories than needed.

Which of these are you already doing?

_____

Which of these will you start today?

_____

'S' is for Sleep.

Make sleep a priority in your family. Aim for 11–14 hours for toddlers, 10–13 hours for preschoolers, 9–11 hours for elementary and junior high schoolers, 8–10 hours for teenagers, and 7–8 hours for adults. Turn off tech devices 1–2 hours before bedtime.

Which of these are you already doing?

_____

Which of these will you start today?

_____

Brain Principle #7
You can change your brain and change your life.

You are not stuck with the brain you have—you can make it better at any age! One of the simplest things you can do is this: before you make any decisions or do anything, ask yourself, **"Is this good for my brain or bad for it?"**

With your help, even young children can learn to do this too! It's so important to work hard to improve your brain health, because with a better brain comes a better mind, better parenting, and a better life.

In the space below, write down three things you recently did that were good for your brain.

1._____

2._____

3._____

Now, write down three things you recently did that were not so good for your brain.

1._____

2._____

3._____

Practice teaching your children to identify what is good for their brain and what is bad for it, and explain the right answer to them. For example, ask them questions such as these:

Questions	Child's Answers
Are blueberries good for your brain or bad for it?	
Is riding a bike with a helmet good for your brain or bad for it?	
Is staying up all night good for your brain or bad for it?	
Is smoking cigarettes good for your brain or bad for it?	
Are walnuts good for your brain or bad for it?	

The Four Circles of Mental Strength

To be mentally strong, your child needs to have a healthy brain, because who they grow up to be is shaped by their brain function. And to be able to parent your children well, you need to have a healthy brain too! Many years ago when I was in medical school, I learned one of the most important lessons of my training: Always think of people as whole beings, not just as their symptoms.

In my practice, I found that optimizing the Four Circles of Mental Strength creates the best outcome for success in all we do in life, and all our children can do and become as adults.

The Four Circles of Mental Strength are:

- **Biological:** how the physical body and brain function
- **Psychological:** developmental issues and thinking patterns
- **Social:** social support and current life situation
- **Spiritual:** connections to God, the planet, past and future generations, and a sense of meaning and purpose

Each of the four circles is comprised of several elements, and each of the elements can have an impact on mental strength. As you review the lists for each of the circles below, place a checkmark next to any item that needs to be improved for you or your child.

BRAIN
Optimize
physical health

MIND
Train it to help
and not hurt

SOCIAL
Managing stress
and relationships

SPIRITUAL
Meaning, purpose,
and why you care

Biological Circle	Parent	Child
Allergies		
Blood Sugar Level		
Brain Health		
Exercise		
Genetics/Family History		
Head Trauma/Injuries		
Hormones		
Hydration		
Infections		
Medications		
Nutrition		
Physical Health		
Sleep		
Supplements		
Toxin Exposure (mold, drugs, alcohol, pesticides, etc.)		

Psychological Circle	Parent	Child
Body Image		
Childhood Development		
Generational History/Issues		
Grief/Loss		
Hope		
Past Failures		
Past Successes		
Self-Concept		
Self-Talk		

	Parent	Child
Sense of Power/Control		
Sense of Self-Worth		
Trauma		
Upbringing		

Social Circle	Parent	Child
Current Successes or Failures		
Finances		
Health Habits of Friends and Family		
Quality of Current Environment		
Relationships		
Sense of Connection to Family, Friends, and Community		
Stressors		
Work/School		

Spiritual Circle	Parent	Child
Connection to a Higher Power		
Connection to Past and Future Generations		
Connection to the Planet		
Morals		
Sense of Meaning and Purpose		
Values		

Which checked items in the Four Circles are of the most concern for you and your child(ren)? What can you do to improve them?

_____

_____

_____

CORE CONVERSATION #2

FOCUSED INTENTION

Your brain makes happen what it sees, so you have to tell your brain what you want—clearly, specifically, and repeatedly.

First, you must ask yourself what kind of parent you want to be, and what type of children you want to raise. Knowing what you want for yourself and for them and discovering what they want in important aspects of their lives helps to clarify goals and leads to more intentional behaviors.

The following tools will help you get clearer about what you want.

Mentally Strong Traits of Children

Place a checkmark next to any of the following traits that you would like your children or grandchildren to develop as they grow up:

- ☐ Confidence
- ☐ Resilience
- ☐ Competence
- ☐ Responsibility
- ☐ Respectfulness
- ☐ Kindness and compassion
- ☐ Resourcefulness
- ☐ Have self-control
- ☐ Be a problem solver
- ☐ Have a generally positive attitude
- ☐ Ability to calm themselves
- ☐ Ability to tolerate discomfort
- ☐ Ability to delay gratification
- ☐ Ability to learn from their mistakes
- ☐ Comfortable asking for help when needed

- ☐ Have healthy relationships
- ☐ Know how to set good boundaries with others
- ☐ Know how to resist temptations from others
- ☐ Have the skills and education necessary to get a job they like that also pays the bills
- ☐ Relate well to others and spend time with quality people
- ☐ Take care of themselves so they are emotionally and physically healthy
- ☐ Live by clearly defined goals and a sense of purpose

From the items you checked above, which ones do you see already developing in your children?

_____

_____

_____

_____

Which of the checked items are not yet apparent in them due to a young age or because of other issues such as behavioral problems or perhaps mixed-messaging from adults?

_____

_____

_____

_____

Goal Setting for Parents and Kids

Instilling motivation, a can-do attitude, and mental strength in children is not quite as difficult as you might think. It starts with setting goals—for yourself and your kids. And, for your goals to be meaningful and effective, you'll first want to identify your sense of purpose, if you do not already know what it is. Whether lofty or humble, each of us has our own sense of purpose, and it is of value.

How to Find Your Sense of Purpose

Answer the following questions to discover your sense of purpose:

1. What do you love to do? What is something you feel qualified to teach others?

_____

_____

2. Who do you do it for? How does your work connect you to others?

_____

_____

3. Are there hurts from your past that you can turn into help for others? Turn your pain into purpose.

_____

_____

4. What do others want or need from you?

_____

_____

5. How do others change as a result of what you do?

_____

_____

6. How do you want to be remembered after you die? What do you want your legacy to be?

_____

_____

** Notice that only a couple of these questions are about you; most of them are about others. Happiness and meaning are often found in helping others.

Establishing Parenting Goals for Yourself and Your Child

Because your mind makes happen what it sees, it is necessary to visualize what you want for yourself as a parent and for your child and then match your behavior to achieve those goals.

In the space below, write 6-8 parenting goals you have for yourself. For example, be loving, kind, a good role model, approachable, etc.

1._____

2._____

3._____

4._____

5._____

6._____

7._____

8._____

In the space below, write 6-8 goals you have for your child. For example, be respectful, self-accepting, resourceful, etc.

1._____

2._____

3._____

4._____

5._____

6._____

7._____

8._____

ONE PAGE MIRACLE FOR PARENTS

To achieve your goals, you must look at them every day. The One Page Miracle, which I give to my own patients to fill out, will help you do just that. Using the template provided, write what you want, not what you don't want, for each of the major areas of your life as a parent. Revise your One Page Miracle over time if your goals change. Put it somewhere you can see it every day and ask yourself, Does it fit? Is my behavior helping me achieve what I want as a parent?"

What do I want for my life as a parent? What am I doing to make it happen?

RELATIONSHIPS

Spouse/Partner: _____

_____

Children: _____

_____

WORK _____

_____

FINANCES _____

_____

SELF _____

_____

Physical: _____

_____

Emotional: _____

_____

Mental: _____

_____

Spiritual: _____

_____

Helping Your Children Set Goals

In addition to having your parenting goals for yourself and your children, it is important to help your kids discover their goals too. However, since it might be hard for them to spontaneously articulate what they want, asking the following questions can prompt them to identify their innermost desires.

1. What do you enjoy doing?

_____

_____

2. What is something you would like to get better at?

_____

_____

3. Is there anything you have never done but would like to try?

_____

_____

4. What would make you happy?

_____

_____

5. How can you show people that you love them?

_____

_____

6. How can you help others who are hurting?

_____

_____

7. What do you think is your purpose in life?

_____

_____

ONE PAGE MIRACLE FOR KIDS

Help your children fill out their own One Page Miracle, or if they are old enough, let them do it themselves. Let them know that this is not homework, but rather a tool that will help make their dreams come true. Be sure to let them know they should write what they want, not what they don't want, and to write in the first person using I statements. Teach your children to ask themselves "Does it fit?" to increase the chances that their behavior and decisions are helping them attain their goals.

What do I want for my life? What can I do to make it happen?

RELATIONSHIPS

Parents: _____

Siblings: _____

Friends: _____

SCHOOL/WORK/CHORES

School: _____

Teachers: _____

Chores/Work: _____

MYSELF

Physical: _____

Emotional: _____

Mental: _____

Spiritual: _____

CORE CONVERSATION #3

BONDING – YOU HAVE NO INFLUENCE WITHOUT CONNECTION

If you want your children to share your values and influence them to be healthy and make good decisions, you must have a strong bond with them. This means you have to make an effort to spend time with them, speak nicely to them, show compassion for their feelings and experiences, and listen to them—really hear what they are saying—even if you don't necessarily agree with them.

The impact of positive bonding provides a multitude of benefits for raising mentally strong kids, including:

- Shared values
- Healthier brain development
- Better ability to cope with stress
- Enhanced learning and life skills
- Reduced risky behaviors

In a nutshell, all healthy relationships require two very important things: time and a willingness to listen. The following strategies will teach you how to strengthen or improve the bonds with your young ones.

Special Time Strategy

In a world that is so often overloaded with to-do lists and electronic distractions, it is too easy to overlook the importance of one-on-one time with a child. For this reason, I recommend this activity to many of the parents I counsel.

Special Time Instructions:

1. Spend 20 minutes a day with your child doing something that they would like to do. This lets children know they are important to you.
2. During special time, do not give any parental commands, questions, or directions. This is not a time for disciplining a child unless they engage in unhealthy behavior.
3. Notice the child's positive behaviors and point them out.
4. Listen more than you talk and be willing to accept and hear what they say.

Special Time Practice (Do this as soon as possible!)

After you have done Special Time with your child or grandchild, answer the following questions about the experience.

1. What activity did the child request you do together?

_____

_____

2. What challenges did you encounter? How was it for you to not direct the activity?

_____

_____

_____

3. What positive behaviors did you notice in your child and share with them?

_____

_____

_____

4. What thoughts or feelings did your child share with you, and how did you reflect them back to the child?

_____

_____

_____

Active Listening Strategy

Helping children know that you value and accept what they think—even if you don't agree with it—helps them feel understood and bolsters their sense of self-efficacy. This, in turn, can improve their ability to make better decisions and solve problems on their own.

There are three simple steps for Active Listening to use when your child is talking to you:

1. Repeat back what you hear without judgment.
2. Listen for the feeling behind the child's words.
3. Reflect back what your child is saying and feeling.

In between each step, give the child space to explain their thoughts, etc. This strategy might be very challenging initially for parents who are more authoritative, but with practice it can help build healthier relationships with your children and and lower the risk of defiant behaviors.

Now it is time to practice this!

Active Listening Practice

In the spaces below, describe your experiences using Active Listening with the child, teen, or young adult in your life. How did it go and what did you learn?

Active Listening Practice #1

_____

_____

_____

_____

_____

_____

Active Listening Practice #2

_____

_____

_____

_____

_____

_____

Active Listening Practice #3

_____

_____

_____

_____

_____

_____

Help for an Active Listening Challenge

Sometimes your kid's view might seem outrageous or make no logical sense to you, and you might be tempted to tune them out or vehemently object. However, if you do, you run the risk of shutting down the conversation. Instead, reflect to them what you heard and add this simple statement:

"I'm not sure that would work for me."

Explain why you wouldn't personally make the choice or decision the child/teen is talking about. This will invite more productive conversation between the two of you.

Now give it a try when you have the opportunity. In the space below describe the experience and what you learned from it.

_____

_____

_____

_____

_____

_____

Effective Parenting Strategy: The 4 Steps to Responsibility

If your child struggles with low self-esteem or has negative notions about themselves, it can be hard for them to believe they are capable or valuable. Fortunately, you can help bolster a more positive sense of self with this simple strategy:

Step 1: Give your child a task they can handle.

Step 2: Hope that they make a mistake or misbehave.

Step 3: Provide sincere empathy and allow them to live with the consequences of their mistake or misbehavior.

Step 4: Give them the same task again.

This exercise teaches children they have the capacity to solve their own problems, which then can improve their confidence and give them a greater sense of self-efficacy.

4 Steps to Responsibility Practice

Describe your experience using this strategy.

Step 1. Task given to child:

_____

Step 2. Child's mistake or misbehavior:

_____

Step 3. How you showed empathy to your child:

_____

Step 4. Results of child's second attempt at the task:

_____

CORE CONVERSATION #4

THE BRAIN NEEDS BOUNDARIES

Firm and loving limits provide guidance and protection as children navigate the complex tasks of growing up. Setting limits teaches them that they are loved and that you care about their well-being in every way.

Healthy limits help them develop responsibility, independence, social skills, academic performance, good behavior, and a decreased risk for mental health or behavioral problems. In other words, appropriate limits and rules support healthy brain development.

However, most parents probably have experienced kids—especially teens—pushing back against limits and rules, sometimes so relentlessly that you caved in from emotional exhaustion.

The following steps will help you stay strong and follow through with what you know is best for your child(ren) when it comes to limits.

6 Steps to Setting Effective Limits

Step 1. Review the goals you have for yourself as a parent and for your child (see Core Conversation #2).

Then, write your answers to the following questions:

What type of adults do you want your kids to become?

_____

_____

What must you consistently model to achieve these goals?

_____

_____

How do you set limits that consistently allow you to support these goals?

_____

_____

How do you consistently follow your goals rather than your short-term feelings?

_____

_____

Next, choose the limits you want to set with your kids. Make sure they are completely enforceable, or they will backfire.

List the limits here:

_____

_____

_____

_____

_____

_____

Step 2. Be prepared for how your kids might react.

When you anticipate their possible responses, it can help you feel less guilty, frustrated, discouraged, or mad if they do react.

What potential reactions might your kids have with the limits you listed above?

_____

_____

_____

_____

_____

_____

Step 3. Learn to neutralize arguing from your kids.

Letting kids talk back, argue, or try to manipulate you does not help anyone. It teaches them how to get their way, deflect responsibility, or get you upset. You can do the following two things to neutralize arguing:

1. Don't overthink or pay much attention to their button-pushing.
2. Respond calmly with a simple one-liner, without using a sarcastic or angry tone. Here are some examples:
    "I love you too much to argue."
    "What did I say?"
    "I know."
    "I'll listen when your voice is calm and respectful."

What is a past example of when your child talked back and argued with you until it wore you down?

_____

_____

_____

How might that exchange be different for both of you if you had known how to neutralize the arguing?

_____

_____

_____

Step 4. Learn to quiet the arguing in your own mind.

Parenting requires clear thinking, but when you're frustrated or upset, your brain produces chemicals that make you feel worse. Conversely, staying level-headed helps you maintain clarity.

When automatic negative thoughts (ANTs) flood your mind about your effectiveness at parenting or setting rules, it's hard to feel optimistic about the changes you're trying to make with regard to setting limits. However, you can practice shifting to more accurate competing thoughts (ACTs) which are not only more realistic, but also can be empowering.

Notice the difference in the tone of the self-talk between ANTs and ACTs in the chart below.

ANTs	ACTs
These new rules aren't working, and they're making my child worse.	These new rules are causing a temporary reaction, but they will pay off in the long run.
I'm a failure as a parent.	I'm doing the best I can, and I'm learning from my mistakes.
Things would be easier if I just let my kid do what they want.	Being permissive will ultimately make my life and my child's life harder.

For Step 4, practice shifting your ANTs to ACTs and notice how much better you feel about the positive changes you're implementing in your household. Record the changes in your thought patterns below:

ANT:_____

ACT:_____

ANT:_____

ACT:_____

ANT:_____

ACT:_____

Step 5. Make sure the limits you set are enforceable.

You must explain them to your kids in an effective and clear manner, otherwise they won't be helpful. For the items below, write down how you plan to enforce them:

- Mean what you say when you give a chore or a direction and be clear that you're willing to back it up with consequences if the child disobeys. How will you convey this to your child?

  _____

- State the direction simply but directly. Give an example of the directions you will use.

  _____

- Give one single direction at a time.

  _____

  _____

- Make sure the child is paying attention when you give the direction. Establish eye contact with them first.

- Be sure you've reduced or removed all distractions in the room.

- If you're not clear if your child has understood the direction, tell them to repeat it back to you.

- If the direction is complex or the child traditionally has trouble doing it the way you like, write down all the steps involved in doing the task. What are some of the steps the child will need for a particular task?

  _____

  _____

  _____

Step 6. Remember that empathy opens the heart and mind to learning.

So, it is important to respond to your child's tantrum with empathy rather than anger. What are some examples of when you responded with anger to your child, and what could you do differently using empathy in the future?

_____

_____

_____

Create a List of Rules for Your Children

It is so important to write down rules for everyone in your household to see and understand. This way, everyone is on the same page with regard to what is acceptable and what is not. In the space below, write out the 8 most important rules for your children.

1. _____
2. _____
3. _____
4. _____
5. _____
6. _____
7. _____
8. _____

For reference, here are the rules that my wife Tana and I have for our home:

Dr. Amen's 8 Essential Rules for Kids

Rule No. 1: Tell the truth.

Rule No. 2: Treat others with respect.

Rule No. 3: Do what Mom or Dad says the first time.

Rule No. 4: No arguing with parents (or grandparents).

Rule No. 5: Respect each other's property.

Rule No. 6: Put away things that you take out.

Rule No. 7: Ask for permission before you go somewhere.

Rule No. 8: Look for ways to be kind and helpful to each other.

CORE CONVERSATION #5

TEACH YOUR KIDS HOW TO SOLVE THEIR OWN PROBLEMS

Most parents want their kids to be happy, comfortable, and fulfilled. However, when parents do too much for them it can interfere with a child's ability to develop the confidence, character, and self-efficacy that help them weather the storms they will encounter throughout their lifetime.

If parents constantly rescue their kids from their own mistakes and missteps they grow up feeling entitled and become self-centered, but they crumble in the face of adversity. These are traits that will not serve them well and can lead to a host of problems, especially in adulthood.

In this section, you will learn and practice some straightforward strategies to help your children learn that they can solve their own problems and feel more effective, confident, and valued as a family member.

Strategy 1. 5 Steps for Guiding Kids to Own and Solve Their Problems

When your child comes to you with a problem they don't want to deal with or are confused about what to do, it is an excellent opportunity to help them learn problem solving. Here are the steps:

Step 1: Provide a strong dose of empathy.
Say something like, "This has got to be so hard."

Step 2: Hand the problem back in a loving way.
Ask, "What do you think you're going to do?"

Step 3: When they reply, "I don't know," ask permission to share what "some kids" decide to do.
Ask, "Would you like to hear what some kids decide to do?"

Step 4: Share two or three options.
Say, "Some kids might decide to _____. Other kids try _____ or _____. How would one of those options work for you?"

Step 5: Allow your child to solve the problem as they see fit.
Say, "I can't wait to hear what you decide. I believe in you!"

Of course, use this process only when problems don't have life-or-death consequences. Once you've had the chance to use this strategy, describe how it went in the space below.

The problem your child brought to you:

_____

Step 1: Empathic statement you made:

_____

Step 2: Child's response when you asked what they were going to do:

_____

Step 3: Was your child open to listening to options that other kids might do?

_____

Step 4: Problem solving options offered to your child, if they were open to suggestions:

_____

Step 5: Results—how did your child decide to solve the problem?

_____

Strategy 2. Help Your Kids Discover Their Sense of Purpose

When people—even children—do things that help others, it provides an important sense of connection and meaningfulness in their lives, and at the same time, reduces feelings of despair, hopelessness, and isolation.

A strong sense of purpose is associated with many benefits including increased happiness and satisfaction, greater self-acceptance, and being emotionally and mentally healthier. Therefore, encouraging your kids, especially teens and young adults, to discover their sense of purpose will serve them well in many aspects of their lives.

Use the steps below to help your child identify what gives them a sense of purpose in life.

5 Steps to Help Kids Find Their Purpose
Talk with your child about what gives you a sense of purpose (remember kids learn from their parents).

_____

_____

Ask your child questions about what's important to them, and write their answers here:

_____

_____

Provide support by sharing your child's enthusiasm for their passions and help them develop those interests. Are there adults you know who might be able to mentor your child? If so, write their names here:

_____

_____

Emphasize the positive impact the child's efforts will have on others and ask them who will benefit from what they enjoy doing.

_____

_____

Have your child create a Purpose Chart using the template on the following page. Once it is complete, put it where they can see it every day.

_____

_____

Purpose Chart

What do I care about?

_____

_____

What are my talents and gifts?

_____

_____

PURPOSE

How do I want to change society/the world?

_____

_____

How do my talents and gifts help others?

_____

_____

Strategy 3. Use Bricks, Not Straw, To Build Strength

From the time they are young, children can begin developing fortitude that will help them get through tough times. The following simple actions, or "Bricks" will give them internal resources to persevere through challenges.

Brick #1: Teach them how to do "stuff"—things that help them feel strong and competent, rather than dependent on others to fix things in their lives, whether it's their home, responsibilities, or issues in other areas of their lives.

In other words, give your kids GUTS (Great Under Trials and Stress). Start by answering these questions for yourself:

What are the specific things I do to keep my family running?

_____
_____
_____

Can my children learn to do these things? _____

How will I teach them?

_____
_____
_____

How can I make much of the learning spontaneous and memorable?

_____
_____
_____

How will I remind myself that the time and effort this requires is well worth it?

_____
_____
_____

Brick #2: Expect them to spend more time creating than "skating."

One of the most effective ways to help kids be successful as they get older is by learning to do as many hard things as possible while growing up. Challenges such as learning to cook or fix things, volunteering in the community, or other actions that push them outside of their comfort zone, build new pathways in the brain that strengthen it.

Answer these questions each week to know if your kids are skating or creating.

1. Have our kids made any sacrifices of time, energy, or other resources to help someone else in a meaningful way, and if so, how?

   _____
   _____
   _____

2. Have our kids created something that takes thought and creativity not just a Google search? What did they do?

   _____
   _____
   _____

3. In what ways have our kids exercised their large muscles? (Physical exercise is critical, not only to strengthen their body, but also for their brain.)

   _____
   _____
   _____

4. Did our kids try anything new this week that they didn't believe they'd be good at, and if so what was it?

   _____
   _____
   _____

5. Did our kids exert a reasonable level of effort when attempting something new, or did they give up right away?

   _____
   _____
   _____

Brick #3: Expect your children to complete chores.

Kids who follow through and do their chores without having to be nagged or bribed are much more likely to become happier and have greater success in school than those who don't. Chores help children develop a stronger bond with their family. By feeling like their contributions are valuable, they are more likely to adopt the family values and less likely to rebel against them and succumb to peer pressure.

To help your children understand all that needs to be done to keep your household running, create a list of responsibilities you can give to them. What are the first 10 things that come to mind?

1._____

2._____

3._____

4._____

5._____

6._____

7._____

8._____

9._____

10._____

Next, let your children choose (within reason) which chores they want to do, and write their names next to those items. If a child refuses to choose, assign chores for them.

Write out the strategy you will use if a child forgets or neglects to complete their chore(s). Remember to use empathy along with the consequence to do the teaching.

_____

_____

_____

Brick #4: Quit your job as entertainment director.

When children are never allowed to experience boredom, it sets the stage for an entitlement to be entertained and diminishes the opportunity for their creativity to develop. To avoid this, try implementing an occasional Boredom Training Session (BTS) using these steps:

Answer these questions each week to know if your kids are skating or creating.

1. Give them lots of items that don't have power cords or use batteries (such as paper, pens, crayons, scraps of wood or fabric, etc.—almost any junk will do). What do you have lying around the house that could work?

    _____

    _____

    _____

2. Schedule a "no-entertainment" hour each week during which TV, phones, and other digital devices, play dates, or other activities are not allowed. Write the day/time for your BTS here.

    _____

    _____

    _____

3. When your child complains about being bored, offer empathy and hand the problem back to the child, encouraging them to experiment and play with the junk you have set out for them. What can you say to them that will help inspire them to do this?

    _____

    _____

    _____

4. Note: If they pitch a fit, don't give into it, but offer empathy and encourage them to get creative once they have calmed down. Write down some words you can use in theses situations.

    _____

    _____

    _____

Brick #5. Teach kids to say no to themselves.

Self-control is essential for being mentally strong, but it is a challenge for all children (and even a lot of adults!). In addition to saying no to a child who asks you about doing something that isn't good for them, you can help them learn to say no to themselves and be more comfortable delaying gratification by teaching them distraction techniques. What are some distraction techniques you already use with your children?

_____

_____

_____

Which of these distractions will be helpful for your child to use?

- ☐ Sing a favorite song.
- ☐ Look in another direction.
- ☐ Tell yourself why it's better to wait.
- ☐ Go for a walk.
- ☐ Think about happy memories.
- ☐ Play a game with someone.

CORE CONVERSATION #6

NOTICE WHAT YOU LIKE ABOUT YOUR KIDS WAY MORE THAN WHAT YOU DON'T

Good mental hygiene is imperative for happiness and success in life. And as parents you must demonstrate this for your children every day, so they can learn from you. Unfortunately, it isn't always easy.

All too often, parents focus on the mistakes children make, or the things they don't like about their kids with the hope that the child will change. However, this often leads to a child developing low self-esteem and growing up with a constant critical dialogue inside their head.

The first step to shifting this unhealthy dynamic is to start paying much more attention to what you like about your child, rather than focus on the things you don't like. In the space below, list positive things about your child:

1._____

2._____

3._____

4._____

5._____

Getting Rid of Automatic Negative Thoughts (ANTs)

A strong negativity bias—or tendency to notice the bad, fearful, or wrong things in others and in oneself—often stems from a regular flow of automatic negative thoughts, or ANTs as I like to call them. Left unchecked these ANTs can lead to mental health struggles with conditions like anxiety and depression as well as inconsistent parenting. Children often suffer silently with ANTs too.

Fortunately, you can learn to eliminate the ANTs in your head and teach your children how to eliminate theirs by regularly doing the exercises in this section. To begin with, review the following list of common ANTs that can adversely affect you and your kids. Place a checkmark next to any that apply.

13 COMMON ANTS

ANT Type	Description	Parent	Child
Just-the-Bad ANTs	A negative filter sees only what's bad in situations.		
Blaming ANTs	Not taking responsibility for your mistakes, or blaming yourself for others' problems		
All-or-Nothing ANTs	Thinking in absolutes, characterized by words such as always, never, no one, everyone, every time, or everything		
Fortune-Telling ANTs	Predicting the worst—even though you have no definite evidence		
Guilt-Beating ANTs	Beating yourself up with words like should, must, ought to, and have to		
Labeling ANTs	Putting negative labels on children (or others), i.e. lazy, dumb, spoiled brat, etc.		
Mind-Reading ANTs	Arbitrarily predict what your child is thinking before you have checked it out.		
Less-Than ANTs	Comparing yourself to others in a negative way		
If-Only and I'll-Be-Happy-When ANTs	Arguing with the past (i.e. dwelling on regrets) or longing for an imaginary future.		
Trust Your Heart ANTs	Not questioning whether a feeling is telling you something true or misleading you		
Want What You Don't Have ANTs	Believing contentment can only be found in a multitude of new and expensive possessions		
Get Even ANTs	Treating someone just as badly, or worse, than they've treated you		
If It Feels Good, Do It—Now! ANTs	Making decisions without considering any long-term consequences		

How to Eliminate the ANTs

This simple strategy will teach you how to challenge and eliminate your ANTs, so you can teach your children how to eliminate theirs too!

Step 1. Whenever you notice a self-critical or distorted thought entering your mind or when you feel sad, mad, nervous, or out of control, identify it and write it down.

Step 2. Identify the type of ANT or negative thought from the list on the previous page and write it down.

Step 3. Talk back to the ANT using these four questions and the Turnaround:

> **Question #1:** Is it true? (Is the stressful or negative thought true?)
> **Question #2:** Is it absolutely true? How do I know with 100 percent certainty?
> **Question #3:** How do I feel when I believe this thought?
> **Question #4:** How would I feel if I didn't have the thought?
> **Turnaround:** Take the original thought and completely turn it around to its opposite, then tell yourself this new version may be true or truer than the original thought.

For younger children, it is best to shorten Step 3 to this:

1. Is it true?
2. Are you 100% sure that [insert negative statement] is true? How do you know?

How to Eliminate the ANTs

Now it's time to practice eliminating the ANTs using the form provided. The more you practice, the better you will become at breaking your old negative thinking habits and developing more rational—and helpful—thinking patterns. Teaching your children to do the same will help them become mentally stronger.

Make copies of this ANT Eliminator Form so you and your children can practice and get better and better at challenging your ANTs and strengthening your Rational Thinking!

ANT Eliminator Form

ANT:_____

ANTType:_____

1. Isittrue?_____

2. Is it 100 percent true? _____

3. How do I feel when I believe this thought? _____

4. How do I feel without the thought? _____

5. Turnaround(oppositethought):_____

Could it be true or truer than the original thought? _____

New thought on which to meditate: _____

PARENTING TIPS TO HELP KIDS CHALLENGE THEIR ANTS

ANT Type	Description
Just-the-Bad ANTs	Help your child develop healthy beliefs about their ability to handle challenges by building up their strengths to help them overcome their areas of weakness.
Blaming ANTs	Make a habit of assuming that most of the unpleasant behavior of others is rooted in their pain, not an intentional plan to rob us of joy.
All-or-Nothing ANTs	Help your child overcome this ANT by asking questions such as, "When was the last time you [insert whatever absolute they are complaining about]?" or "Do you remember when . . . ?"
Fortune-Telling ANTs	If your child tends to predict the future, have them write or say phrases that are more rational and realistic.
Guilt-Beating ANTs	When your kids say phrases like, "I should..." or "I need to..." help them rephrase their thoughts to more empowering words such as, "I want to...", "I choose to...", or "It fits my goals to..."
Labeling ANTs	When kids label themselves (or another child), help them understand that making a mistake or doing something naughty doesn't make them stupid, bad, lazy, etc. Brainstorming reasons for a person's behavior can also help increase empathy.
Mind-Reading ANTs	Making assumptions about others often leads to miscommunication and misunderstanding. Teach your child the phrase, "If I don't know, say so" when they aren't sure what a person is thinking or why they did something.
Less-Than ANTs	Make sure you aren't comparing your kids to their siblings, friends, or classmates. Teach them that instead of trying to be "the best" it's healthier to "be their best."
If-Only and I'll-Be-Happy-When ANTs	To combat this ANT, teach your children gratitude, and practice it every day at home.
Trust Your Heart ANTs	Acknowledge your child's feelings but help them question whether the feeling is telling you something true or if it is misleading them.
Want What You Don't Have ANTs	Be sure you're modeling contentment and appreciating what you have, so that your kids will learn from your positive attitude.
Get Even ANTs	Create a home where you treat others better than they treat you. This Bible quote is a great reminder: "Do not be overcome by evil, but overcome evil with good." (Romans 12:21, ESV).
If It Feels Good, Do It—Now! ANTs	Ask your child one of my favorite questions, "Then what?" and ask it a few more times to see if the choice that seems to feel good in the moment will also feel good later and be good for their brain.

CORE CONVERSATION #7

GET KIDS HELP EARLY WHEN THEY NEED IT

If you have been implementing the strategies in this workbook but have a child who is still struggling with school, misbehaving, having conflicts with others, problems with friends, or other issues outside the norm, it may be due to an undiagnosed brain health problem.

If so, your child is not alone. There are more than 73 million children aged 17 and younger who have brain health problems—psychiatric or learning disorders—in the U.S. However, sometimes it is hard for parents to discern normal from abnormal behavior because of the way in which childhood development shifts over time.

The following checklists of common mental health issues and symptoms can provide valuable information to share with your pediatrician. If warranted, the doctor might refer you to a psychiatrist or other mental health professional to get help for your child. When that is the case, it is highly recommended you follow through as soon as possible to help your child.

ADHD Symptoms in Kids

- ☐ Inattention
- ☐ Being disruptive in class
- ☐ Picking fights with siblings or schoolmates
- ☐ Easily distracted
- ☐ Waits until the last minute to start chores or homework
- ☐ Misses deadlines
- ☐ Chronic lateness
- ☐ Messy room and desk
- ☐ Doesn't learn from mistakes
- ☐ Impulsivity
- ☐ In constant motion—fidgeting, jumping, roughhousing

Anxiety Symptoms in Kids

- ☐ Frequently feeling anxious or nervous
- ☐ Excessive worrying
- ☐ Being easily startled
- ☐ Avoids conflict
- ☐ Heightened muscle tension
- ☐ Headaches and stomachaches
- ☐ Being excessively shy or timid
- ☐ Easily embarrassed

Depression Symptoms in Kids

- ☐ Feeling sad, hopeless, or helpless
- ☐ Lack of interest in hobbies or activities they used to enjoy
- ☐ Feeling fatigued
- ☐ Changes in appetite—eating substantially more or less food than usual
- ☐ Sleeping a lot more or less than usual
- ☐ Difficulty concentrating
- ☐ Appearing to lack motivation
- ☐ Having body aches and pains
- ☐ Irritability
- ☐ Engaging in self-destructive or self-injurious behavior (including suicidal thoughts and behaviors)

Obsessive-Compulsive Disorder (OCD) Symptoms in Kids

- ☐ Obsessive thoughts
- ☐ Compulsions—counting, excessive handwashing, etc.
- ☐ Excessive or senseless worrying
- ☐ Overfocused tendencies
- ☐ Oppositional—their favorite word is no
- ☐ Argumentative
- ☐ Holding grudges
- ☐ Getting upset when things don't go their way
- ☐ Unhealthy perfectionism
- ☐ Being upset when things are out of place

PANDAS and PANS

If you're not familiar with these acronyms, they stand for pediatric autoimmune neuropsychiatric disorders associated with streptococcal infections (PANDAS), which are a subset of pediatric acute-onset neuropsychiatric syndrome (PANS). These are mental health and behavioral problems that occur suddenly in children following one of these bacterial or viral infections:

(Check any that your child has had)

- ☐ Strep
- ☐ Mononucleosis
- ☐ Lyme disease
- ☐ Epstein Barr virus
- ☐ Mycoplasma pneumoniae (walking pneumonia)

PANS/PANDAS Symptoms in Kids

- ☐ OCD
- ☐ Restrictive eating
- ☐ Intense anxiety, panic attacks, or new phobias
- ☐ Inattention and/or hyperactivity
- ☐ Vocal or motor tics
- ☐ Depression and/or suicidal thoughts and behaviors
- ☐ Anger or aggression
- ☐ Oppositional behavior
- ☐ Sensory sensitivities
- ☐ Behavioral regression
- ☐ Decline in math and handwriting abilities
- ☐ Trouble sleeping
- ☐ Bedwetting
- ☐ Symptoms associated with autism
- ☐ Psychosis
- ☐ Decrease in school performance

Adverse Childhood Experiences (ACEs)

Traumatic events in your life or your child's can increase the risk for mental health issues and medical problems down the road. If you were exposed to trauma while growing up, it can make parenting challenges more stressful.

Identifying your ACE score and getting help for yourself if warranted, as well as knowing a child's ACE score can provide direction for treatment that can reduce the risk of suffering in silence.

Take the ACE Questionnaire to get your scores.

ACE Questionnaire

Please answer Yes or No to each question for yourself and for your child to get an idea of how trauma may be impacting you.

1. Before your 18th birthday, did a parent or other adult in the household often or very often swear at you, insult you, put you down, or humiliate you? Or act in a way that made you afraid that you might be physically hurt? You _____ Your child _____

2. Before your 18th birthday, did a parent or other adult in the household often or very often push, grab, slap, or throw something at you? Or ever hit you so hard that you had marks or were injured? You _____ Your child _____

3. Before your 18th birthday, did an adult or person at least five years older than you ever touch or fondle you or have you touch their body in a sexual way? Or attempt to or have oral, anal, or vaginal intercourse with you? You _____ Your child _____

4. Before your 18th birthday, did you often or very often feel that no one in your family loved you or thought you were important or special? Or your family didn't look out for each other, feel close to each other, or support each other?
You _____ Your child _____

5. Before your 18th birthday, did you often or very often feel that you didn't have enough to eat, had to wear dirty clothes, and had no one to protect you? Or your parents were too drunk or high to take care of you or take you to the doctor if you needed it? You _____ Your child _____

6. Before your 18th birthday, was a biological parent ever lost to you through divorce, abandonment, or other reason? You _____ Your child _____

7. Before your 18th birthday, was your mother or stepmother often or very often pushed, grabbed, slapped, or had something thrown at her? Or sometimes, often, or very often kicked, bitten, hit with a fist, or hit with something hard? Or ever repeatedly hit for at least a few minutes or threatened with a gun or knife? You _____ Your child _____

8. Before your 18th birthday, did you live with anyone who was a problem drinker or alcoholic, or who used street drugs? You _____ Your child _____

9. Before your 18th birthday, was a household member depressed or mentally ill, or did a household member attempt suicide? You _____ Your child _____

10. Before your 18th birthday, did a household member go to prison? You _____ Your child _____

Scoring

Add up the number of yes responses you have and your child has and enter it here: You _____ Your child _____These are your ACE scores.

21 TIPS FOR GRANDPARENTS

TO HELP RAISE MENTALLY STRONG KIDS

If you have grandchildren, you know that being a part of their lives is one of the greatest blessings. You get to enjoy the myriad benefits of spending time with the "grands" and watching them grow up, while also enriching their lives with your presence, guidance, wisdom, and love.

Whether it is time spent together on the weekends, during school vacations, babysitting, or afternoon play dates, you have the opportunity to bond with them in meaningful ways and be a positive influence on their development. And while that time might not always be free of challenges, the following do's and don'ts can help you make the most of the relationships you have with your grandkids and their parents.

1. Don't speak badly about your grandkids' parents.
Never tell your grandkids things like, "Your mom and dad are parenting all wrong" or "Don't listen to your parents because they don't know what they're doing." This confuses kids and shows a lack of respect for their parents. Showing a united front in terms of raising children is the best strategy.

2. Do teach your grandkids about your household rules.
From an early age, let the grands know that your home has unique rules, so they learn to respect them as they grow up. Simple things, such as taking off shoes in the mudroom or not jumping on the beds, helps kids understand that different houses can have different rules that they must adhere to.

3. Do make sure you follow through with the same discipline practices their parents use.
Whether it's time-out or no TV for an hour after misbehaving, it's important to be consistent with consequences.

4. Don't spoil them.
Avoid the temptation to shower them with too many presents, otherwise you will set unrealistic expectations for them as they grow up.

5. Do have healthy snacks available.
Make sure you have foods like nut butters, fruit, and fresh veggies with hummus that support a child's brain function. Avoid having bowls of candy that will give them a sugar rush, drain their brain power, and make them cranky later. That's no fun for either of you.

6. Do set boundaries regarding babysitting.
If you enjoy babysitting your grandchildren, make sure you set healthy boundaries around your availability. Otherwise, parents may take advantage of you, which can lead to feelings of resentment.

7. Do teach your grandkids new games.
Make it a point to show the grands how to play board games or card games that they don't yet know. And ask them to teach you how to play their favorite games or help you get better at digital technology.

8. Do share your hobbies.
If a grandchild shows interest in one of your hobbies, take the time to teach them how to do it.

9. Don't be a pushover.
Be alert for the tried-and-true childhood trick of, "When Mom or Dad says no, ask Grandma and Grandpa..." If your grandchild tries to talk you into allowing them to do something they aren't usually allowed to do, get permission from their parents before you agree to it.

10. Do spend one-on-one time together.
Plan an occasional outing with each grandchild individually to help them know they are special to you and create memories that both of you will cherish.

11. Do read to them.
Take time to read books to young grandchildren and let them practice reading to you so they can boost their language skills.

12. Do show an interest in things they enjoy.
Make an effort to learn what their interests are and what things are important to them. Ask questions about school and activities they enjoy and spend time doing things they like to do.

13. Don't be tech illiterate.
Understand that technology is an everyday part of their world but set boundaries around that in your home. For example, you may want to make a rule about no phones at the table during meals.

14. Do be their cheerleader.
If your grandchildren play sports, go to their games when you can, or if they are in choir or theater go to their performances and let them know how proud you are of their effort and abilities.

15. Do assign household chores.
Ask the grandkids to pitch in with age-appropriate chores to help them learn responsibility.

16. Do remember these two words: firm and kind.
When a child misbehaves, be firm but kind with discipline to help them understand the consequences of their actions, rather than using harsh words and making them feel ashamed of their missteps.

17. Don't tell your adult children how to parent their kids.
This is a common and often well-intentioned—but very annoying—habit many grandparents have. Unless a child is emotionally or physically endangered, offer your parenting advice only when it is solicited.

18. Do stay connected, no matter how far away you are.

If you live far away from your grandkids, you can still be a part of their lives by sending cards, talking to them on the phone or via video, sharing pictures, or seeing them on social media. Staying connected, even at a distance, helps them get to know you, and vice versa.

19. Do teach your grandchildren about your family history.

Share unusual or historic facts specific to their ancestors. This helps them develop a deeper connection to past generations.

20. Don't be too demanding about spending time with your grandkids.

Remember that when you were a young parent, your lives were likely filled to the brim. And accept that at some point, your grands will naturally switch their focus to their friends and activities. It doesn't mean they don't care about you. It simply means they are going through the developmental stages of becoming more independent and growing up—just as all of us once did.

21. Do be a good role model.

Always keep in mind that they are watching you—that you are a role model for them—so make sure your words and actions match, and that your behavior is teaching them what is acceptable and what is not.

NOTES